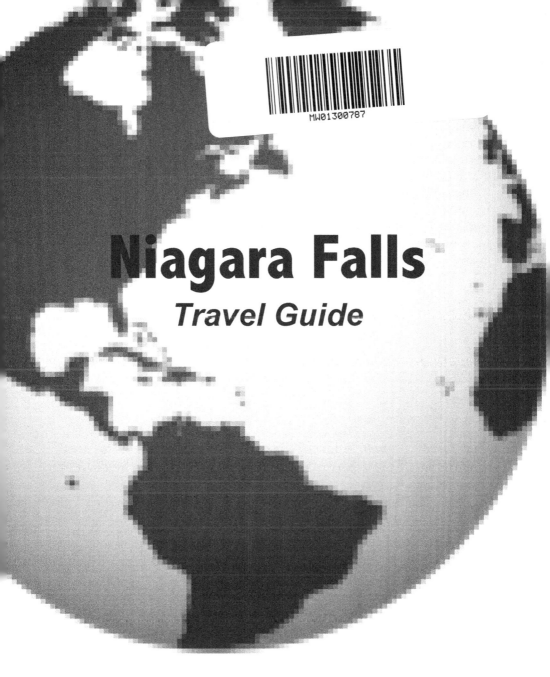

Niagara Falls
Travel Guide

Quick Trips Series

No part of this publication may be reproduced, stored in a retrieval system, or transmitted, in any form or by any means without the prior written permission of the publisher, nor be otherwise circulated in any form of binding or cover other than that in which it is published and without similar condition being imposed on the subsequent purchaser. If there are any errors or omissions in copyright acknowledgements the publisher will be pleased to insert the appropriate acknowledgement in any subsequent printing of this publication. Although we have taken all reasonable care in researching this book we make no warranty about the accuracy or completeness of its content and disclaim all liability arising from its use.

Copyright © 2016, Astute Press
All Rights Reserved.

Table of Contents

NIAGARA FALLS 6
- CUSTOMS & CULTURE 9
- GEOGRAPHY 11
- WEATHER & BEST TIME TO VISIT 15

SIGHTS & ACTIVITIES: WHAT TO SEE & DO 17
- NIAGARA FALLS STATE PARK 17
  - Maid of the Mist (Boat Trip) 19
  - Journey Behind the Falls 20
  - Cave of the Winds 21
  - Whirlpool Aero Cars...22
- NIAGARA FALLS BOTANICAL GARDENS & BUTTERFLY CONSERVATORY 23
- BIRD KINGDOM 25
- NIAGARA FALLS HISTORY MUSEUM 26
- "IMAGINE" MAGIC SHOW (GREG FREWIN THEATRE) 27
- FALLSVIEW INDOOR WATER PARK..28
- HERSCHELL CARROUSEL FACTORY MUSEUM 29
- GRAPE & WINE TOURS 31
- CASINOS 32
  - Seneca Casino 32
  - Fallsview Casino Resort 33
  - Casino Niagara..33
- OLD FORT NIAGARA..34

BUDGET TIPS 36

🌐 ACCOMMODATION 36
 Greystone Manor 36
 Super 8 37
 Holiday Inn 38
 Skyline Inn 39
 Yogi Bear's Camp Jellystone 40

🌐 PLACES TO EAT 41
 Flying Saucer Restaurant 41
 Jimmy Buffett's Margaritaville 43
 Bob Evans 43
 Buzz's New York Style Pizza 44
 Two Favorites for Snacks 45
 Twist O' the Mist 45
 Beavertails Pastry 46

🌐 SHOPPING 47
 Three Sisters Trading Post 47
 Duty Free Americas 48
 Skylon Tower 49
 Niagara Falls Fashion Outlets 50
 Hershey's Niagara Falls 50

KNOW BEFORE YOU GO 52

🌐 ENTRY REQUIREMENTS 52

🌐 HEALTH INSURANCE 53

🌐 TRAVELING WITH PETS 54

🌐 AIRPORTS 56

🌐 AIRLINES 60

🌐 HUBS 63

🌐 SEAPORTS 65

🌐 MONEY MATTERS 67

- Currency 67
- Banking/ATMs 67
- Credit Cards 68
- Tourist Tax 69
- Sales Tax 70
- Tipping 71
- Connectivity 72
- Mobile Phones 72
- Dialing Code 74
- Emergency Numbers 74
- General Information 74
- Public Holidays 74
- Time Zones 75
- Daylight Savings Time 77
- School Holidays 77
- Trading Hours 78
- Driving 78
- Drinking 80
- Smoking 81
- Electricity 82
- Food & Drink 83
- American Sports 85
- Useful Websites 87

NIAGARA FALLS TRAVEL GUIDE

Niagara Falls

Niagara Falls (located on both sides of the Canada/United States border) has been a popular honeymoon destination since the Civil War. That romantic tradition continues today and New York State and Ontario proudly proclaim Niagara Falls the "Honeymoon Capital of the World".

NIAGARA FALLS TRAVEL GUIDE

Niagara Falls offers something for everyone. In addition to the world-famous waterfalls there are interesting museums and gardens as well as family-oriented camping and waterparks.

There are two areas of Niagara Falls – one in the United States (New York) and one in Canada in the province of Ontario. The Canadian side is generally thought of as the most scenic and impressive and the spray from the Falls can be felt from quite a distance.

The United States side is the oldest designated state park in the United States and shouldn't be ignored. In fact, visitors to the United States side can actually get closer to the Falls. The two sides more or less blend into one another so it's easy to experience both during a visit.

NIAGARA FALLS TRAVEL GUIDE

The Niagara River moves into Lake Erie, which in turn spills into Lake Ontario and these water sources combine to create the force of water pressure that creates the Falls. There are three waterfalls in Niagara. The largest one is Horseshoe Falls, on the Canadian side and is an impressive 2600 feet wide. The American Falls and Bridal Veil Falls are both in the United States and are about 1060 feet width. Niagara Falls is located 17 miles from Buffalo, New York and about 75 miles from Toronto, Canada.

The waterfall effect was created back at the end of the Ice Age, when existing glaciers melted and receded. Some of the glaciers helped form the Great Lakes and others changed direction to go toward the Niagara River, carving out a section of rocky land heading toward the Atlantic Ocean.

NIAGARA FALLS TRAVEL GUIDE

Three areas of rock formations were involved and they didn't erode in the same way or at the same time, because they were made of varying amounts of limestone and dolostone. It took years for the full erosion effect to be complete, as chunks of stone gave way.

The name Niagara is Mohawk for "neck of the river" which was once called o-ne-au-ga-rah.

Tourists first began visiting the area in the 1800s, though it was still in a primitive state. The Falls soon became an international topic of conversation and Jerome Bonaparte, brother of Napoleon Bonaparte, visited in the early 19th century.

NIAGARA FALLS TRAVEL GUIDE

Over time, attractions of all types sprung up, along with lodging and restaurants. Marilyn Monroe and Joseph Cotton filmed "Niagara" at the Falls in the 1950s and Princess Diana visited the area as have several U.S. Presidents while in office.

🌎 Customs & Culture

It's debatable who discovered Niagara Falls. A Frenchman named Samuel de Champlain explored the area in 1604 and members of his team saw the Falls, which he then wrote about in his journal.

In 1642, a French Jesuit priest named Rev. Paul Ragueneau wrote in his journal about discovering the area. In 1677 a Belgian man named Louis Hennepin, a missionary, also claimed to discover the Falls.

NIAGARA FALLS TRAVEL GUIDE

The first detailed and scientific documentation took place in the early 18th Century when Pehr Kalm, a naturalist of Finnish and Swedish descent documented his findings.

Tourists began visiting the area as word of the discoveries took place and soon there was a demand for a way to cross from the United States to the Canadian side and back again. A suspension bridge was built. Additional bridges were constructed in 1886, 1897 and 1941. This last bridge, called the Rainbow Bridge, is a primary means for cars and people to travel to and from Niagara Falls to this day.

In addition to the romance of the area, Niagara Falls has earned a more unusual reputation as a place for daredevils. Going over the Falls in a barrel has been a risky stunt as early as 1829, as has plunging over the

NIAGARA FALLS TRAVEL GUIDE

Falls into the water. Some brave souls have been successful in their attempts, while many have not.

In addition to the raw beauty of the rushing water three casinos with slot machines, gaming tables and Las Vegas-style entertainment have been built nearby. There are also botanical gardens, floral exhibits, parks offering glimpses of birds, butterflies or sea creatures, numerous wineries, and several military locations and forts, relating to the area's heavy involvement in the War of 1812.

The area's beauty and history are best explored outdoors. It's free to view the Falls but many visitors opt for one or more additional experiences that provide a more adventurous or up-close look as though one is immersed in the midst of the waters.

NIAGARA FALLS TRAVEL GUIDE

No matter what language one speaks, or where one's country of origin is, the sight of the raging waters – beyond anything seen anywhere else – can unite people in sheer awe and wonder.

🌐 Geography

Niagara Falls, New York and Niagara Falls, Ontario are joined by the Rainbow Bridge, which is a toll bridge, with tolls averaging less than a dollar.

The Buffalo-Niagara International Airport, in Buffalo, New York accommodates the largest selection of airlines and is the primary gateway. It's located about 30-40 minutes from either Niagara Falls location and most major airlines fly here.

NIAGARA FALLS TRAVEL GUIDE

The smaller but closer Niagara Falls Airport serves primarily charter planes though connecting flights from Spirit Airlines and Allegiant Air arrive here as well.

Once at the airport, the ITA Shuttle runs to either the Canadian or U.S. side for about $45 per person to the U.S. side or $55 per person to Canada. Call 716-630-6000 for more information.

The Buffalo Airport Shuttle (716-685-2550) can accommodate a family of four for about $22 per person and the drivers are known for offering helpful hints about the area.

Amtrak (800-USA-RAIL) makes a stop at the Niagara Falls station for those arriving by train. There is also a bus depot (905-357-2133) near the Falls and from there a taxi

NIAGARA FALLS TRAVEL GUIDE

ride to the Falls costs about $10-15. Visitors who have spent time in New York City or Boston often extend their vacation by taking a bus tour to the Falls offered by companies like www.TakeTours.com

It's possible to rent a car at the airport but parking at various attractions can be expensive. If driving into Niagara Falls, the final freeway before arriving would be the I-190. After crossing the South Grand Island Bridge, immediately take Exit 21 to the Robert Moses Parkway, until it becomes Prospect Street. From there, signs will direct you to Niagara Falls.

The Falls Shuttle Bus offers an all-day pass for $10 and stops at many locations in the area. The WeGo Bus operates around town and stops at many points of

NIAGARA FALLS TRAVEL GUIDE

interest. A one-day pass for ages 13+ is $7 and ages 6-12 pay $4. Ages two and under are free.

A People Mover bus system offers a day pass for $7.50 adults, $4.50 children. Buses run every 20 minutes and cover much of the area around the Falls.

Tickets on the Niagara Transit System are available in the immediate area of the Falls. A day pass for an adult and two children averages $6.

After visitors have arrived downtown near the Falls, many attractions are best experienced on foot.

Please note that even for United States and Canadian citizens, a passport is needed when crossing the border from the U.S. to Canada and back. Those from other

NIAGARA FALLS TRAVEL GUIDE

countries may need a visa. Travelers should check the Canada Border Services Agency (www.cbsa-asfcgc.ca) for information, travel tips and entry requirements.

There is no waiting period for a marriage license in Niagara Falls. Pay the $100 fee at the City Clerk's Office and the first hurdle toward matrimony has been overcome. The office is at 4310 Queen Street or call 905-356-7521, extension 4283 for information. No weddings are performed at this location, however.

If you are on honeymoon, pick up an official Honeymoon Certificate at the Niagara Falls Tourism Office which will give you special discounts at area attractions.

NIAGARA FALLS TRAVEL GUIDE

Here is a searchable map of Niagara Falls and area attractions: http://maps.google.com/?11=43.099506,-79008742&spn=0.128851,0.307617&t=m&z=12

🌎 Weather & Best Time to Visit

Niagara Falls is open year-round and visitors can view them in all weathers. From November through March some of the up-close viewing platforms are closed and many museums or outdoor attractions have limited schedules.

The most pleasant time to visit is from May through October when the weather is warmer. The early spring months of March to April could experience snow. Average temperatures will be from 1° C (34° F) to 14° C (57° F), perhaps slightly higher in May.

NIAGARA FALLS TRAVEL GUIDE

Summer (from June through August) is warm during the day but still comfortable at night. It's definitely shorts and t-shirt weather for the most part. Temperatures will range from 19° C to 27°C (80° F) or more.

In the fall months of September – November, the leaves start change color and it can be a beautiful time to visit. Temperatures avearge 16° C (62° F) to 4° C (40° F) and rain is common in late October to November.

The winter months of December through February are often icy and cold. Temperatures are known to drop to freezing level or below. The average temperatures are -1° C (30° F) to -4° C (24° F) with some days even colder.

NIAGARA FALLS TRAVEL GUIDE

To see today's weather in Niagara Falls see:

http://www.wunderground.com/cgi-bin/findweather/hdfForecast?query=Niagara+Falls+NY

NIAGARA FALLS TRAVEL GUIDE

Sights & Activities: What to See & Do

🌐 Niagara Falls State Park

716-278-1796

www.niagarafallsstatepark.com

Viewing the three Niagara Falls is free and merely pulling into a parking lot or disembarking from your taxi or tour bus is all that is required. You may walk up to a railing and take in the entire area. The Canadian side gives you

NIAGARA FALLS TRAVEL GUIDE

the best perspective on all three falls. For many, this sight in itself is enough to satisfy as the sight is so magnificent. The sight and sound of the rushing water, the mist rising even from far away, and the rainbow that often forms over the water on a sunny or partly sunny day, is awe-inspiring.

There are additional options you might want to consider as well. Packages include: the Discovery Pass, priced at $33.00 Adults, $26 ages 6-12 and those under 6 are free. This package offers a 35% savings, on admission to the Cave of the Winds, Niagara Discovery Center, Maid of the Mist, Niagara Adventure Theatre, and the Aquarium of Niagara. Packages change each season so check the park website when planning your trip.

Another web site, www.niagarafallstourism.com, offers an Adventure Pass for $19.75 adults, $12.65 for ages 6-12,

NIAGARA FALLS TRAVEL GUIDE

with ages 5 and under free. This offers savings on admission to the Maid of the Mist, White Water Walk, $3 off at the Butterfly Conservatory, $2 off the Aero Car, food discounts, $5 off a $30 purchase at any Niagara Parks store plus two-day transport passes on the People Mover.

Individual information on the major Falls-related experiences is listed below. Two helpful hints – use waterproof cameras on any of these excursions because water will hit your camera! And visit in the early morning or late afternoon to avoid waiting in potentially long lines.

Maid of the Mist (Boat Trip)

5920 Niagara Parkway at Prospect Point

Niagara Falls, New York 14303

716-284-8897

Board at Queen Victoria Park, Maid of the Mist Plaza, on

NIAGARA FALLS TRAVEL GUIDE

River Road

www.niagarafallstourism.com

Besides the view of Niagara Falls, this is arguably the most popular attraction. The Maid of the Mist boat trip has been a tourist attraction since 1846. Princess Diana, Marilyn Monroe, Mikhail Gorbachev and Brad Pitt are a few celebrities who have experienced this ride. It offers visitors the chance to ride in a boat to actually "look up" at Niagara Falls.

Open from late April to the end of October, two 600-passenger boats depart every 15 minutes for a 30-minute ride that sails towards the Falls – so close, in fact, that souvenir raincoats are handed out free with admission, to partially protect visitors from the guaranteed splashes of

NIAGARA FALLS TRAVEL GUIDE

water. Tickets are $15.50 for ages 13+, $9 for ages 6-12. Ages 5 and under are free.

Journey Behind the Falls

6650 Niagara Parkway

Niagara Falls, Ontario, Canada L2E 6T2

905-351-0254

Journey begins at the Table Rock Welcome Centre

www.niagaraparks.com

At Journey Behind the Falls, an elevator takes visitors 150 feet below the Falls to an observation deck at the foot of Niagara Falls. This is a way to see the massive waterfalls from behind, as the name implies. Free rain ponchos are distributed because there will considerable splashes of water. Admission from April through December is $15.95 for adults and $10.95 for children 6-12. Children under 5 are free. This attraction is open in winter months but the lowest observation deck is closed due to ice, so admission is $11.25 for adults and $6.95 for ages 6-12. The winter hours are from 9 a.m. to 5 p.m. M-F, till 6 p.m. Spring and Fall hours are 9 a.m. – 7 p.m. weekdays, till 8 p.m. on weekends. Summer hours are daily from 9 a.m. till 10 or 11 p.m. depending on crowds.

Cave of the Winds

Goat Island, Niagara Falls, New York 14303

716-278-1730

www.niagaraparks.com

This is the closest visitors can get to the Falls. Visitors board an elevator to descend 175 feet down into the Niagara Gorge, and then take wooden walkways along

NIAGARA FALLS TRAVEL GUIDE

the river gorge to Hurricane Rock, just a few feet from the rushing water.

Bridal Veil Falls is the closest waterfall and it creates lots of spray so souvenir rain ponchos and special sandals are dispensed with the price of admission. Adult tickets are $11, ages 6-12 are $8 and under 5 are free. Open in early May from 9 a.m. – 5 p.m., weekends till 7 p.m. Summer hours are 9 a.m. till 9 p.m., with weekends till 10 p.m. From Sept. 3 till late October, open 9 a.m. till 7 p.m. Monday – Friday and on Sunday; Saturday closing is 9 p.m.

Whirlpool Aero Cars

3850 Niagara River Parkway

Niagara Falls, Ontario, Canada L2E 3E8

877-642-7275

NIAGARA FALLS TRAVEL GUIDE

www.niagaraparks.com

These antique cable cars ascend into the air as the water rushes below. When the water changes direction as the 10-minute ride advances, it creates a whirlpool effect. The attraction has been operating since 1916. Tickets are $13.50 for adults, ages 6-12 tickets are $8.50; no charge for children under age five. The attraction is closed in winter. It opens in April with hours of 10 a.m. – 5 p.m. on weekdays. In the summer, it is open 9 a.m. till 8 p.m. daily. In the fall, hours are the same as in the spring.

🌐 Niagara Falls Botanical Gardens & Butterfly Conservatory

2565 Niagara Parkway

Niagara Falls, Ontario, Canada L2E 3G4

NIAGARA FALLS TRAVEL GUIDE

905-356-8554

www.niagaraparks.com

This tranquil location was established in 1936 and is about 5 miles from Niagara Falls. The Botanical Gardens offer 99 acres of gardens, featuring a section of shade trees and plants, vegetables, an expansive herb garden and a rose garden with about 2400 roses. There is also an arboretum with trees such as pine, fir, elm, birch and maple. There are seasonal displays and the greenhouse also changes displays. Admission is free and the gardens are open from May to October from dawn to dusk. Visitors wishing to take a horse and carriage tour of the gardens may purchase tickets for $18.50 person.

One of the main points of interest within the gardens is the Butterfly Conservatory, actually a separate attraction worthy of visiting. More than 2000 tropical butterflies, representing 45 species, fly freely within the greenery of the conservatory. Paths meander through the tropical rain forest setting. Tours are self-guided and include a section where it's likely that you'll see new butterflies emerge from cocoons. There is an admission to the conservatory. Adult tickets are $13.50, ages 6-12 are $8.50 and children under 5 visit free. The conservatory is open year-round though the hours vary. From January to June and from October – December, it opens at 10 a.m. and closes at 5p.m. In the summer (June through September) it is open from 10 a.m. to 7 or 8 p.m. (dusk). Call 877-642-7275 for additional information.

Bird Kingdom

5651 River Road

Niagara Falls, Ontario, Canada L2E 7M7

NIAGARA FALLS TRAVEL GUIDE

866-994-0090

www.birdkingdom.ca

The Bird Kingdom is home to the largest indoor aviary in the world where birds fly free. Over 400 exotic birds representing countries around the world fly in 9 different areas. Visitors can feed the birds as well as hold them (Lorikeets, for example). There is a small bird aviary. The main section is a 50,000 square foot tropical rainforest setting including a 40-foot waterfall – not quite Niagara Falls but still beautiful! There is also a reptile encounter area. In the Discovery Zone, guests can meet handlers of the reptiles and birds.

Admission is $13 for adults, $11 for seniors and $9 for children. Open June 30 till September 1 from 9:30 a.m. till

5 p.m. It's best to leave a coat or jacket behind since it can be very warm due to the tropical climate indoors.

🌎 Niagara Falls History Museum

5810 Ferry Street

Niagara Falls, Ontario, Canada L2G 1S9

905-358-5082

www.niagarafallsmuseums.ca

Located in the old Stamford Town Hall and built in 1874, the museum contains three galleries telling the Niagara Falls story. Relics such as guns, buttons, and archives from the War of 1812 are featured at the museum as well as photos and items pertaining to the geology of the area.

There are usually special exhibits and recent ones have included a mock 1850s tavern and a Gift of the Nile

NIAGARA FALLS TRAVEL GUIDE

exhibit. Adult admission is $5, ages 7-19 are $4, children 6 and under are admitted free. The museum is open year-round. Hours Tuesday, Wednesday and Sunday are 10 a.m. – 5 p.m. and Thursday 10 a.m. to 9 p.m. Within steps from the museum lies the Drummond Hill Cemetery, worthy of a visit to pay homage to the remains of those who fought in the bloody battle of 1812.

"Imagine" Magic Show (Greg Frewin Theatre)

5781 Ellen Avenue

Niagara Falls, Ontario, Canada L2G 3P8

866-870-3002

www.gregfrewintheatre.com

This 600-seat dinner theatre, located just minutes from

NIAGARA FALLS TRAVEL GUIDE

the Falls, features a Las Vegas-style magic show that is considered a "must-see" by locals and visitors alike.

Magician Greg Frewin comes here after long-standing performances in other venues such as Las Vegas, the Bahamas and Malaysia. Dinner is served at 6:15 p.m. and the show begins at 7:30 p.m. Tickets range from $45 - $60 for adults and from $27.50 - $35 for children, depending on location. There is a no-dinner option for those wanting to see the show only. Tickets are $35 for adults and $25 for ages 4-12. Seating is at the back of the theatre but visibility is still good.

Fallsview Indoor Water Park

5685 Falls Ave., Niagara Falls, Ontario L2E 6W7

888-234-8408

www.niagarafallsstatepark.com

NIAGARA FALLS TRAVEL GUIDE

Located across from Niagara Falls near to the Rainbow Bridge, in the heart of the tourist district, the Fallsview Indoor Water Park provides three acres of water-related fun for all ages. Sixteen slides are available as well as a wave pool, plunge bowl, a tiny tot area, a 1000-gallon tipping bucket, a play area, a sundeck, an adults-only area, a Jacuzzi and a pool. A day pass costs $45.

Herschell Carrousel Factory Museum

180 Thompson Street, North Tonawanda, NY 14120

716-693-1885

www.carrouselmuseum.org

The Herschell Carrousel Factory Museum is 15 minutes drive outside of town and it offers a nice change of pace.

NIAGARA FALLS TRAVEL GUIDE

It is a national historic site. Carousels (merry-go-rounds) are a part of most American childhoods.

This location has been the most famous and prolific maker of carousels since 1915 and the carousels were created right on this spot, and are shipped from here to carnivals or amusement parks.

The buildings – all original – can be visited. They show the entire process of making a merry-go-round. In one building, there are over 20 hand-carved animals and photos that date back many years, showing the creative process of making the horses, pigs and other animals. The woodcarving building shows the art of carving a carousel horse from a piece of wood. The Wurlitzer building shows the music rolls used in providing the distinctive carousel music.

NIAGARA FALLS TRAVEL GUIDE

A main part of the visit is the two vintage merry-go-rounds. There's a kiddie carousel from the 1940s, safe enough for even small children to ride while their parents watch. The larger carousel is from 1916 and is one of the first completed after the factory began production. There are 36 horses on the ride, with the outer ring made in 1916 style and the inner ring representing the style of the 1890s. Nearly 600 lights illuminate the carousel. There are other rides for small children to enjoy, as well.

Admission is $6 for adults. $3 for children ages 2-16. Admission includes one ride token – additional tokens are available for 50 cents. The museum is closed from January 2 – April 2. From April 3-June 14 and from September 4 through December 30 it is open from 12-4 p.m. Wednesday-Sunday. From June 15 through

NIAGARA FALLS TRAVEL GUIDE

September 3, it is open from 10 a.m. to 4 p.m. Monday – Saturday and Sunday from 12 to 4 p.m.

🌐 Grape & Wine Tours

758 Niagara Stone Road

Niagara-on-the-Lake, Ontario, Canada L0S 1J0

866-562-9449

www.infoniagara.com

With the emphasis clearly placed on the Falls, many are unaware that just 15 minutes from Niagara Falls there are at least 25 vineyards producing fine wines. The Grape & Wine Tours company provides an "Afternoon Delight" tour of small wineries that produce fine, award-winning wines. Guests are picked up and returned to their accommodation and tour three wineries with the aid of a tour guide. They have the opportunity to meet with a winemaker and tastings are definitely a fun part of the experience. The 3-winery experience takes place from 1:30 to 4:30 p.m. and costs $65 per adult. A Lunch Fiesta Tour featuring a gourmet lunch and tour of 4 wineries with tastings is $95 and lasts from 10:30 a.m. to 4:30 p.m. Pick-up and return also included.

Casinos

Three casinos have been added to the Niagara Falls experience in the past few years, offering gaming and entertainment for adults. They have become highly popular with locals and tourists and are located within walking distance of the Falls.

Seneca Casino

310 Fourth Street

Niagara Falls, New York 14303

NIAGARA FALLS TRAVEL GUIDE

877-873-6322

www.senecaniagaracasino.com

This casino is located at the Rainbow Bridge area. It offers nearly 2600 slot machines, 91 gaming tables, restaurants and name entertainers such as Aretha Franklin, Eddie Money, Seth Meyers, Tony Orlando, Judy Collins, Vanessa Williams and Leon Russell have performed in the showroom.

Fallsview Casino Resort

6380 Fallsview Boulevard

Niagara Falls, Ontario, Canada L2G 7X5

888-325-5788

www.fallsviewcasinoresort.com

This large casino offers 3000 slot machines, 130 gaming

tables, a poker room plus the Avalon Theatre, where names such as Bette Midler, Styx, Richard Marx, Diana Krall, Hank Williams, Jr. and Sophia Loren (in a lecture format) have entertained in the past. There are shops on the premises, as well.

Casino Niagara

5705 Falls Avenue

Niagara Falls, Ontario, Canada L2G 6T3

888-946-3255

www.casinoniagara.com

Located close to the Falls, this casino offers slots, gaming tables, a comedy club, live music, off-track betting, sports betting and blackjack tables.

🌍 Old Fort Niagara

Youngstown Lockport Road at Fort Niagara State Park

Youngstown, New York 14174

716-745-7611

www.oldfortniagara.org

This location is about 15-20 minutes from the heart of the Falls and is worth visiting for the historical significance. It has more than 300 years of military history. During the Colonial Wars it controlled access to the Great Lakes. From 1825 onward its function as a guard post was less needed but it remained active as a military post until 1963.

Three flags (French, British and American) fly at the Fort, representing the three nations that held possession of the Fort at various times. The British were in possession of

NIAGARA FALLS TRAVEL GUIDE

the Fort until the War of 1812, when they ceded it to the United States. During both World Wars, the Fort served as barracks and training center for soldiers. Today the U.S. Coast Guard is the only military presence.

Tours are available from 9 a.m. daily year-round, closing at 5 p.m. except from June to September, when it is open till 7 p.m. Adult admission is $12, children 6-12 are admitted for $8, ages 5 and under are admitted free. Senior and AAA discounts are available.

NIAGARA FALLS TRAVEL GUIDE

Budget Tips

 Accommodation

Greystone Manor

4939 River Road, Niagara Falls, Ontario, Canada L2E 3G6

905-357-7373

www.greystone-manor.ca

NIAGARA FALLS TRAVEL GUIDE

Built in 1908, this onetime mansion was turned into a bed and breakfast in 1988.

It recently underwent a careful restoration. The manor offers a view of the riverbanks and is within brief walking distance of the Falls, casinos and many major attractions. Among the amenities offered: WiFi, TVs, DVD players, air conditioning, and hairdryers. A complete breakfast is served beginning at 9 a.m. It includes an ever-changing selection of fruits, breads, egg dishes and pancakes or waffles plus beverages. Rooms are $115-125 nightly.

Super 8

5706 Ferry Street

Niagara Falls, Ontario, Canada L2G 1S7

888-442-6095

www.super8niagarafalls.com

NIAGARA FALLS TRAVEL GUIDE

Affordable lodging is offered with Internet access, in-room coffeemakers, small refrigerators, air conditioning, plus they are pet friendly and cribs are available. Guests receive a $5 voucher daily toward breakfast at the on-site restaurant and a $15 dinner voucher for Mama Mia's restaurant in the Fallsview Casino. There is an on-site shuttle to the Falls or it is a comfortable 15-minute walk away. Rooms start at $69.

Holiday Inn

5339 Murray Street

Niagara Falls, Ontario, Canada L2G 2J3

800-263-9393

www.holidayinnniagarafalls.com

Slightly higher but still affordable prices of $119-149 and

NIAGARA FALLS TRAVEL GUIDE

could go to $295 depending on date of arrival and number of people in the party, but there are many advantages.

The property is family-oriented and is very close to the Falls, near the Skylon Tower (with its observation deck, shops and restaurants) and casinos, and it offers on-site laundry facilities, a spa, gift shop, tour booking desk, pool and restaurant. Honeymoon rooms with a private whirlpool are available and a honeymoon package from $132-295 features dinner for two in Skylon Tower, dinner for two at nearby Coco's Restaurant, breakfast, 15% off souvenirs, and wine tasting at a nearby winery.

Skyline Inn

4800 Bender Street

Niagara Falls, Ontario, Canada L2G 3K1

800-263-7135

NIAGARA FALLS TRAVEL GUIDE

www.skylineniagarafalls.com

This property is connected to the Fallsview Water Park and is close to the Falls plus Hershey's World, a huge chocolate store.

Several restaurants such as the Hard Rock Café, Perkins and Planet Hollywood are nearby. Perkins and Planet Hollywood are part of a hotel package where, when adults pay $149 for the room/meal package, children can eat free – one child per adult.

Rooms feature air conditioning, TV, Internet, a small refrigerator, wake-up calls, iron and ironing board, in-room coffeemaker. They also have family night movies in the courtyard. The Skyline has a special on a room with 2 Queen-sized beds from $66 – 100 and a King bedroom is

$120. A family suite for up to 6 people, including a separate sleeping area for parents runs from $166.

Yogi Bear's Camp Jellystone

8676 Oakwood Drive

Niagara Falls, Ontario, Canada L2E 6S5

800-558-2954, code 5 connects to the Niagara Falls property

Park grounds open from 8 a.m. – 11 p.m. daily

www.jellystoneniagara.com

Open seasonally from April 20 – October 15, this property is fun for adults but it might just be one of the highlights of a vacation for children. It's located just minutes from the Falls and many other major attractions.

NIAGARA FALLS TRAVEL GUIDE

There are many options here, from RV camping to tent sites, from trailers to cottages and cabins. Tents run $37-43 a night. A "Boo-Boo" deluxe cabin, named after a character in the Yogi cartoons, is a nicely appointed cabin and runs $120-135 a night. The Yogi Cottage is $130-155 nightly. Cabins and cottages feature air conditioning, TV, bath, kitchen and are like a full-service motel room. For guests in tents, there are nearby bathrooms. The area has many fire pits and picnic tables near the sleeping grounds.

The extras at this location are impressive – a souvenir shop, laundry facilities, a snack bar, playground, wagon rides, a game room, campfire activities, mini golf and a chance for the kids to meet Yogi and Boo-Boo.

NIAGARA FALLS TRAVEL GUIDE

🌐 Places to Eat

Flying Saucer Restaurant

6768 Lundy's Lane

Niagara Falls, Ontario, Canada L2G 1V5

905-356-4553

www.flyingsaucerrestaurant.com

Great fun for everyone! This restaurant was built to look just like a "flying saucer", especially the take-out section. Indoors, "aliens" sit in booths, and there are mysterious colored lights.

It's a family restaurant with good, reasonable food. They have a breakfast special for just $1.99 from 6 a.m. to 2 p.m. that includes eggs, fries, and toast. Other menu items for breakfast include omelettes, egg dishes, pancakes and waffles. Lunch and dinner selections include sandwiches, soups and salads, chicken, seafood, fajitas, hot dogs, burgers, and platters consisting of a sandwich, fries and cole slaw. Most items on the menu run from $4.99 to $19.99. Open from 6 a.m. – 3 a.m. daily and weekends from 6 a.m. to 4 a.m.

Jimmy Buffett's Margaritaville

6300 Fallsview Boulevard

Niagara Falls, Ontario, Canada L2G 7T8

905-354-1245

www.margaritavilleniagara.ca

Guests can party in an island setting at this restaurant that's part of a chain. Live music plus karaoke nightly and in spite of the rather adult theme to the song the restaurant name is based on, this can be a couple's night out or a family restaurant, complete with a kids' menu. Vegetable platters, burgers, salads, baby back ribs, jerk chicken and pasta are a few items offered. Most items are priced between $9-25. They are open Monday – Friday from noon – midnight, and on Saturday and Sunday from 11:30 a.m. to midnight.

Bob Evans

6543 Niagara Falls Boulevard

Niagara Falls, New York 14304

716-283-2965

www.bobevans.com

This is a family-owned restaurant that prides itself on inexpensive but tasty family food, using fresh and local ingredients. They offer pasta, burgers, soup, chicken, meat loaf, chicken pot pie, ribs among other items and

NIAGARA FALLS TRAVEL GUIDE

there are always several 3-course specials featuring a starter, entrée and dessert for $9.99. Most choices on the menu are under $12.

Buzz's New York Style Pizza

7617 Niagara Falls Boulevard

Niagara Falls, New York 14304

716-283-5333

www.buzzsnypizza.com

This restaurant features Italian food at affordable prices. Pizza, of various types, is a favorite. Other items include subs, calzones, spaghetti, soup or salad.

A small pizza averages $8.95 with additional toppings at $1.25. Spaghetti with bread is $6.75. Calzones are $9.75. There are several lunch specials including 3 slices of pizza and a drink for $4.75, or a sub sandwich, fries and drink for $7.50 and soup, or a salad and a drink for $7.95. They are open 7 days a week, Sunday – Thursday from 11 a.m. to 11 p.m. and Friday and Saturday from 11 a.m. till midnight.

Two Favorites for Snacks

There are two locations in the area that attract locals and visitors for specialized snacks or light "bites". They have both become a "must" on the list of travelers.

Twist O' the Mist

18 Niagara Street

Niagara Falls, New York 14303

716-285-0702

https://www.facebook.com/pages/Twist-o-the-Mist/215466558515787

This is "the" place in the area for ice cream, and you won't have to look hard to find it since the entire building is shaped like a giant ice cream cone. It's also close to the Falls. It's open all summer from 11 a.m. to 11 p.m. and offers 72 flavors of ice cream!

Beavertails Pastry

4967 Clifton Hill

Niagara Falls, Ontario, Canada L2G 3N5

290-296-2056

www.beavertailsinc.com

This unusual pastry cafe has become a classic with visitors and locals. Even President Obama stopped by to try one when he visited the area in 2009. The beaver is one of Canada's best-known national symbols and this wholewheat pastry is hand-strctched until it resembles the tail of a beaver. It is then topped with a never-ending supply of choices, and served hot. Some people choose chocolate/banana, while others go for the cinnamon/sugar variety. There are peanut butter toppings, M&Ms, chocolate/hazelnut – it's an individual choice.

Smoothies, beverages and yogurt are also on the menu. The prices run from $5-12. From May to August Beavertails is open daily from 11 a.m. till anywhere up to midnight, if they are busy. They are open from September to October on Mondays – Thursdays from 12 noon till 10 p.m., Friday from noon till midnight, Saturday 11 a.m. till midnight and Sunday 11 a.m. till 10 p.m. Limited opening hours from November till April – Closed except for the weekends – Friday noon to midnight, Saturday 11 a.m. till midnight and Sunday 11 a.m. till 8 p.m.

🌐 Shopping

Three Sisters Trading Post

454 Main Street

Niagara Falls, New York 14301

716-284-3689

www.threesisterstradingpost.com

The three sisters who own this large, Native American-themed store and café say their location's motto is "not just a store – an experience." The rustic-looking outside log building sets the tone and when Howie, the Talking Moose greets visitors at the door, it promises fun. The store specializes in items made by local artisans such as dream catchers, jewelry, clothing, home accessories and other gifts and collectibles. They are also proud to offer tourist-related items such as t-shirts and sweatshirts, cameras, batteries, postcards, inexpensive souvenir clothing and much more. There is an on-site café/snack bar for hungry shoppers, too. The store is open from 9 a.m. – 5 p.m. daily.

Duty Free Americas

Rainbow Bridge Plaza

Niagara Falls, New York 14303

716-284-9736

www.dutyfreeamericas.com

Visitors who are leaving the U.S. for more than 48 hours can purchase luxury items and save 10-50%. Those items include cosmetics, fragrances and skin care (with labels like Lancome, Chanel, Prada, Gucci, Calvin Klein and Dior), cookies and candy, luxury gifts by Victoria's

Secret, Armani, Coach, Guess and Hermes, tobacco and wine and spirits. Open 24 hours daily during summertime.

Skylon Tower

5200 Robinson Street

Niagara Falls, Ontario, Canada L2G 2A3

888-975-9566

www.skylon.com

Whether visitors are serious about shopping or just want to browse, it's worth a stop at the Skylon Tower, 775 feet above Niagara Falls. The Observation Deck costs $11 for adults. There is a buffet dining room offering lunch with an observation deck ticket as a package (prices are $27.50 adults and children $12.50). Shopping is another option at the substantial mini-mall that offers international boutiques, Canadian souvenirs, jewelry, and crafts and art by local artisans.

Niagara Falls Fashion Outlets

1900 Military Road

Niagara Falls, New York 14304

716-297-0933

www.fashionoutletsniagara.com

Tourists should visit at least one shopping outlet while on vacation. This one will satisfy everyone with 150 stores such as Saks, Michael Kors, Brooks Brothers, Coach, Kate Spade, Banana Republic and many more. Open 10 a.m. – 9 p.m. on Monday – Saturday and on Sunday from 11 a.m. – 6 p.m.

NIAGARA FALLS TRAVEL GUIDE

Hershey's Niagara Falls

5701 Falls Avenue Suite 400

Niagara Falls, Ontario, Canada

800-468-1714

www.hersheycanada.com

Chocolate and candy-lovers should allow time to visit Hershey's at Niagara Falls. Enter through the giant replica of a Hershey's bar that's 4 stories tall, have your photo taken with a giant Hershey's Kiss, sample the candy, the chocolate-dipped strawberries or a milkshake. Shop for chocolate cookies, specialty items, collectibles, cookbooks and Hershey's candy. Visit from 10 a.m. to 5 p.m. daily.

NIAGARA FALLS TRAVEL GUIDE

Know Before You Go

Entry Requirements

The Visa Waiver Programme (VWP) allows nationals of selected countries to enter the United States for tourism or certain types of business without requiring a visa. This applies to citizens of the UK, Australia, New Zealand, Canada, Chile, Denmark, Belgium, Austria, Latvia, Estonia, Finland, Italy, Hungary, Iceland, France, Germany, Japan, Spain, Portugal, Norway, Sweden, Slovenia, Slovakia, Switzerland, Brunei, Taiwan, South Korea, Luxemburg, Singapore, Liechtenstein, Monaco, Malta, San Marino, Lithuania, Greece, the Netherlands and the Czech Republic. To qualify, you will also need to have a passport with integrated chip, also known as an e-Passport. The e-Passport symbol has to be clearly displayed on the cover of the passport. This secure method of identification will protect and verify the holder in case of identity theft and other breaches of privacy. There are exceptions. Visitors with a criminal record, serious communicable illness or those who were deported or refused entry on a past occasion will not qualify for the Visa Waiver Program and will need to apply for a visa. Holders of a UK passport who have dual citizenship of Iraq, Iran, Sudan, Syria, Somalia, Libya or Yemen (or those who have travelled to the above countries after 2011) will also need to apply for a visa. A requirement of the Visa Waiver Programme is online registration with the Electronic System for Travel Authorisation (ESTA) at least 72 hours before your travels. When entering the United States, you will be able to skip the custom declaration and proceed directly to an Automated Passport Control (APC) kiosk.

If travelling from a non-qualifying country, you will need a visitor's visa, also known as a non-immigrant visa when entering the United States for visiting friends or family, tourism or medical procedures. It is recommended that you schedule your visa interview at least 60 days before your date of travel. You will need to submit a passport that will be valid for at least 6 months after your intended travel, a birth certificate, a police certificate and color photographs that comply with US visa requirements. Proof of financial support for your stay in the United States is also required.

Health Insurance

Medical procedures are very expensive in the United States and there is no free or subsidized healthcare service. The best strategy would be to organize temporary health insurance for the duration of your stay. You will not need any special vaccinations if visiting the United States as tourists. For an immigration visa, the required immunizations are against hepatitis A and B, measles, mumps, rubella, influenza, polio, tetanus, varicella, meningococcal, pneumococcal, rotavirus, pertussis and influenza type B.

There are several companies that offer short-term health insurance packages for visitors to the United States. Coverage with Inbound USA can be purchased online through their website and offer health insurance for periods from 5 to 364 days. Visitor Secure will provide coverage for accidents and new health complications from 5 days to 2 years, but the cost and care of pre-existing medical conditions and dental care is excluded. Inbound Guest offers similar terms for periods of between 5 and 180 days and will email you a virtual membership card as soon as the contract is finalized. Physical cards will be available within one business day of arrival to the United States.

Traveling with Pets

The United States accepts EU pet passports as valid documentation for pets in transit, provided that your pet is up to date on vaccinations. In most instances, the airline you use will require a health certificate. While microchipping is not required, it may be helpful in case your pet gets lost. If visiting from a non-English speaking country, be sure to have an English translation of your vet's certificate available for the US authorities to examine. To be cleared for travel, your pet must have a vet's certificate issued no less than 10 days before your date of travel. Pets need to be vaccinated against rabies at least 30 days prior to entry to the United States. If the animal was recently microchipped, the microchipping procedure should have taken place prior to vaccination. In the case of dogs, it is also important that your pet must test negative for screwworm no later than 5 days before your intended arrival in the United States.

In the case of exotic pets such as parrots, turtles and other reptiles, you will need check on the CITES (Convention on International Trade in Endangered Species of Wild Fauna and Flora) status of the breed, to ensure that you will in fact be allowed to enter the United States with your pet. There are restrictions on bringing birds from certain countries and a quarantine period of 30 days also applies for birds, such as parrots. It is recommended that birds should enter the United States at New York, Los Angeles or Miami, where quarantine facilities are available. The owner of the bird will carry the expense of the quarantine and advance reservations need to be made for this, to prevent the bird being refused entry altogether. Additionally, you will need to submit documentation in the

NIAGARA FALLS TRAVEL GUIDE

form of a USDA import permit as well as a health certificate issued by your veterinarian less than 30 days prior to the date of entry.

Airports

Your trip will probably be via one of the country's major gateway airports. **Hartsfield–Jackson Atlanta International Airport** (ATL), which is located less than 12km from the central business area of Atlanta in Georgia is the busiest airport in the United States and the world. It processes about 100 million passengers annually. Internationally, it offers connections to Paris, London, Frankfurt Amsterdam, Dubai, Tokyo, Mexico City and Johannesburg. Domestically, its busiest routes are to Florida, New York, Los Angeles, Dallas and Chicago. Delta Airlines maintains a huge presence at the airport, with the largest hub to be found anywhere in the world and a schedule of almost a thousand daily flights. Via a railway station, the airport provides easy access to the city.

Los Angeles International Airport (LAX) is the second busiest airport in the United States and the largest airport in the state of California. Located in the southwestern part of Los Angeles about 24km from the city center, it is easily accessibly by road and rail. Its nine passenger terminals are connected through a shuttle service. Los Angeles International Airport is a significant origin-and-destination airport for travellers to and from the United States. The second busiest airport in California is **San Francisco International Airport** (SFO) and, like Los Angeles it is an important gateway for trans-Pacific connections. It serves as an important maintenance hub for United and is home to an aviation museum. Anyone who is serious about green policies and environmentally friendly alternatives will love San Francisco's airport. There is a special bicycle route to the airport, designated bicycle parking zones and even a service that offers special freight units for travelling with your bicycle. Bicycles are also allowed on its Airtrain service. The third airport of note in California is **San Diego International Airport** (SAN).

Chicago O'Hare International Airport (ORD) is located about 27km northwest of Chicago's central business district, also known as the Chicago Loop. As a gateway to Chicago and the Great Lakes region, it is the US airport that sees the highest frequency of arrivals and departures. Terminal 5 is used for all international arrivals and most international departures, with the exception of Air Canada and some airline carriers under the Star Alliance or Oneworld brand. The Airport Transit System provides easy access for passengers between terminals and to the remote sections of the parking area.

NIAGARA FALLS TRAVEL GUIDE

Located roughly halfway between the cities of Dallas and Fort Worth, **Dallas-Fort Worth International Airport** (DFW) is the primary international airport serving the state of Texas. Both in terms of passenger numbers and air traffic statistics, it ranks among the ten busiest airports in the world. It is also home to the second largest hub in the world, that of American Airlines, which is headquartered in Texas. Through 8 Interstate highways and 3 major rail services, it provides access to the city centers of both Dallas and Fort Worth, as well as the rest of Texas. An automated people mover, known as the Skylink makes it effortless for passenger to transverse between different sections of the airport and the parking areas. Terminal D is its international terminal. The second busiest airport in Texas is the **George Bush Intercontinental Airport** (IAH) in Houston, which offers connections to destinations across the United States, as well as Mexico, Canada, the Americas and selected cities in Europe and Asia.

John F. Kennedy International Airport (JFK) is located in the neighborhood of Queens. In terms of international passengers, it is one of the busiest airports in the United States, with connections to 6 continents and with the air traffic of 70 different airlines. Its busiest routes are to London, Paris, Los Angeles and San Francisco. It serves as a gateway hub for both Delta and American Airlines. Terminal 8, its newest terminal, is larger than Central Park. It has the capacity of processing

NIAGARA FALLS TRAVEL GUIDE

around 1600 passengers per hour. An elevated railway service, the Airtrain provides access to all 8 of its terminals and also connects to the Long Island railroad as well as the New York City Subway in Queens. Within the airport, the service is free. Three other major airports also service the New York City area. **Newark Liberty International Airport** (EWR) is New York's second busiest airport and home of the world's third largest hub, that of United Airlines. Newark is located about 24km from Mid Manhattan, between Newark and Elizabeth. Its airtrain offers an easy way of commuting around the airport and connects via the Newark Liberty International Airport Station to the North Jersey Coast line and Northeast Corridor line. Other airports in New York are **La Guardia Airport** (LGA), located on the Flushing Bay Waterfront in Queens and **Teterboro Airport** (TEB), which is mainly used by private charter companies.

Washington D.C. is served by two airports, **Baltimore-Washington International Airport** (BWI) and **Washington Dulles International Airport** (IAD). Other important airports on the eastern side of the United States include **Logan International Airport** (BOS) in Boston, **Philadelphia International Airport** (PHL) and **Charlotte Douglas International Airport** (CLT) in North Carolina. The three busiest airports in the state of Florida are **Miami International Airport** (MIA), **Fort Lauderdale-Hollywood International**

NIAGARA FALLS TRAVEL GUIDE

Airport (FLL) and **Tampa International Airport** (TPA). In the western part of the United States, **McCarran International Airport** (LAS) in Las Vegas and **Phoenix Sky Harbor International** (PHX) in Arizona offer important connections. **Denver International Airport** (DEN) in Colorado is the primary entry point to Rocky Mountains, while **Seattle-Tacoma International Airport** (SEA) in Washington State and **Portland International Airport** (PDX) in Oregon provide access to the Pacific Northwest. **Honolulu International Airport** (HNL) is the primary point of entry to Hawaii.

Airlines

The largest air carriers in the United States are United Airlines, American Airlines and Delta Airlines. Each of these could lay claim to the title of largest airline using different criteria. In terms of passenger numbers, Delta Airlines is the largest airline carrier. It was founded from humble beginnings as a crop dusting outfit in the 1920s, but grew to an enormous operation through mergers with Northeast Airlines in the 1970s, Western Airlines in the 1980s and North-western Airlines in 2010. Delta also absorbed a portion of Pan Am's assets and business, following its bankruptcy in the early 1990s. Delta Airlines operates Delta Connections, a regional service covering North American destinations in Canada, Mexico and the United

NIAGARA FALLS TRAVEL GUIDE

States. In terms of destinations, United Airlines is the largest airline in the United States and the world. Its origins lie in an early airline created by Boeing in the 1920s, but the company grew from a series of acquisitions and mergers - most recently with Continental Airlines - to its current status as a leading airline. Regional services are operated under the brand United Express, in partnership with a range of feeder carriers including CapeAir, CommutAir, ExpressJet, GoJet Airlines, Mesa Airlines, Republic Airlines, Shuttle America, SkyWest Airlines and Trans State Airlines. American Airlines commands the largest fleet in the United States. It originated from the merger of over 80 tiny regional airlines in the 1930s and has subsequently merged with Trans Caribbean Airways, Air California, Reno Air, Trans World Airlines and, most recently, US Airways. Through the Oneworld Airline Alliance, American Airlines is partnered with British Airways, Finnair, Iberia and Japan Airlines. Regional connections are operated under the American Eagle brand name and include the services of Envoy Air, Piedmont Airlines, Air Wisconsin, SkyWest Airlines, Republic Airlines and PSA Airlines. American Airlines operates the American Airlines Shuttle, a service that connects the cities of New York, Boston and Washington DC with hourly flights on weekdays.

Based in Dallas, Texas, Southwest Airlines is the world's largest budget airline. It carries the highest number of domestic

NIAGARA FALLS TRAVEL GUIDE

passengers in the United States and operates over 200 daily flights on its 3 busiest routes, namely Chicago, Washington and Las Vegas. JetBlue Airways is a budget airline based in Long Island that operates mainly in the Americas and the Caribbean. It covers 97 destinations in the United States, Mexico, Costa Rica, Puerto Rico, Grenada, Peru, Colombia, Bermuda, Jamaica, the Bahamas, Barbados, the Dominican Republic and Trinidad and Tobago. Spirit Airlines is an ultra low cost carrier which offers flights to destinations in the United States, Latin America, Mexico and the Caribbean. It is based in Miramar, Florida.

Alaska Airlines was founded in the 1930s to offer connections in the Pacific Northwest, but began to expand from the 1990s to include destinations east of the Rocky Mountains as well as connections to the extreme eastern part of Russia. Alaska Airlines recently acquired the brand, Virgin America which represents the Virgin brand in the United States. Silver Airways is a regional service which offers connections to various destinations in Florida, Pennsylvania, Virginia and West Virginia and provides a service to several islands within the Bahamas. Frontier Airlines is a relatively new budget airline that is mainly focussed on connections around the Rocky Mountain states. Hawaiian Airlines is based in Honolulu and offers connections to the American mainland as well as to Asia. Island Air also serves Hawaii and enjoys a partnership with

NIAGARA FALLS TRAVEL GUIDE

United Airlines. Mokulele Airlines is a small airline based in Kona Island. It provides access to some of the smaller airports in the Hawaiian Islands. Sun Country Airlines is based in Minneapolis and covers destinations in the United States, Mexico, Costa Rica, Puerto Rica, Jamaica, St Maarten and the US Virgin Islands. Great Lakes Airline is a major participant in the Essential Air Service, a government programme set up to ensure that small and remote communities can be reached by air, following the deregulation of certified airlines. These regional connections include destinations in Arizona, Colorado, Kansas, Minnesota, Nebraska, New Mexico, South Dakota and Wyoming. In the past, Great Lakes Airline had covered a wide range of destinations as a partner under the United Express banner.

Hubs

Hartsfield Jackson Atlanta International Airport serves as the largest hub and headquarters of Delta Airlines. John F. Kennedy International Airport serves as a major hub for Delta's traffic to and from the European continent. Los Angeles International Airport serves as a hub for Delta Airline's connections to Mexico, Hawaii and Japan, but also serves the Florida-California route. Detroit Metropolitan Wayne County Airport is

NIAGARA FALLS TRAVEL GUIDE

Delta's second largest hubs and serves as a gateway for connections to Asia.

Washington Dulles International Airport serves as a hub for United Airlines as well as Silver Airways. United Airlines also use Denver International Airport, George Bush Intercontinental Airport in Houston, Los Angeles International Airport, San Francisco International Airport, Newark Liberty International Airport and O'Hare International Airport in Chicago as hubs.

Dallas/Fort Worth International Airport serves as the primary hub for American Airlines. Its second largest hub in the southeastern part of the US is Charlotte Douglas International Airport in North Carolina and its largest hub in the north is O'Hare International Airport in Chicago. Other hubs for American Airlines are Phoenix Sky Harbor International Airport - its largest hub in the west - Miami International Airport, Ronald Reagan Washington National Airport, Los Angeles International Airport, John F Kennedy International Airport in New York, which serves as a key hub for European air traffic and La Guardia Airport also in New York.

Seattle-Tacoma International Airport serves as a primary hub for Alaska Airlines. Other hubs for Alaska include Portland International Airport, Los Angeles International Airport and Ted Stevens - Anchorage International Airport. Virgin America operates a primary hub at San Francisco International Airport, but also has a second hub at Los Angeles International Airport as well as a significant presence at Dallas Love Field. Denver International Airport is the primary hub for Frontier Airlines, which also has hubs at Chicago O'Hare International Airport and Orlando International Airport. Frontier also maintains a strong presence at Hartsfield-Jackson Atlanta International Airport, Cincinnati/North Kentucky International Airport, Cleveland Hopkins International Airport, McCarran International Airport in Las Vegas and Philadelphia International Airport. Honolulu International Airport and Kahului Airport serve as hubs for Hawaiian Airlines. Mokulele Airlines uses Kona International Airport and Kahului Airport as hubs. Minneapolis–Saint Paul International Airport serves as a hub for Delta Airlines, Great Lakes Airlines and Sun Country Airlines. Silver Airways uses Fort Lauderdale-Hollywood International Airport as a primary hub and also has hubs at Tampa International Airport, Orlando International Airport and Washington Dulles International Airport.

Seaports

The Port of Miami is often described as the cruise capital of the world, but it also serves as a cargo gateway to the United States. There are 8 passenger terminals and the Port Miami Tunnel, an

NIAGARA FALLS TRAVEL GUIDE

undersea tunnel connects the port to the Interstate 95 via the Dolphin Expressway. Miami is an important base for several of the world's most prominent cruise lines, including Norwegian Cruise Lines, Celebrity Cruises, Royal Caribbean International and Carnival Cruises. In total, over 40 cruise ships representing 18 different cruise brands are berthed at Miami. Well over 4 million passengers are processed here annually. There are two other important ports in the state of Florida. Port Everglades is the third busiest cruise terminal in Florida, as well as its busiest cargo terminal. It is home to *Allure of the Seas* and *Oasis of the Seas*, two of the world's largest cruise ships. Oceanfront condominium dwellers often bid ships farewell with a friendly cacophony of horns and bells. The third important cruise port in Florida is Port Canaveral, which has 5 cruise terminals.

With its location on the Mississippi river, New Orleans is an important cargo port, but it also has a modern cruise terminal with over 50 check-in counters. The Port of Seattle is operated by the same organization that runs the city's airport. It has two busy cruise terminals. The Port of Los Angeles has a state of the art World Cruise Center, with three berths for passenger liners. As the oldest port on the Gulf of Mexico, the Port of Galveston dates back to the days when Texas was still part of Mexico. Galveston serves both as a cargo port and cruise terminal.

NIAGARA FALLS TRAVEL GUIDE

Money Matters

Currency

The currency of the United States is US dollar (USD). Notes are issued in denominations of $1, $2, $5, $10, $20, $50 and $100. Coins are issued in denominations of $1 (known as a silver dollar, 50c (known as a half dollar), 25c (quarter), 10c (dime), 5c (nickel) and 1c (penny).

Banking/ATMs

ATM machines are widely distributed across the United States and are compatible with major networks such as Cirrus and Plus for international bank transactions. Most debit cards will display a Visa or MasterCard affiliation, which means that you may be able to use them as a credit card as well. A transaction fee will be charged for withdrawals, but customers of certain bank groups such as Deutsche Bank and Barclays, can be charged smaller transaction fees or none at all, when using the ATM machines of Bank of America. While banking hours will vary, depending on the location and banking group, you can generally expect most banks to be open between 8.30am and 5pm. You will be asked for ID in the form of a passport, when using your debit card for over-the-counter transactions.

NIAGARA FALLS TRAVEL GUIDE

While you cannot open a bank account in the United States without a social security number, you may want to consider obtaining a pre-paid debit card, where a fixed amount can be pre-loaded. This service is available from various credit card companies in the United States. The American Express card is called Serve and can be used with a mobile app. You can load more cash at outlets of Walmart, CVS Pharmacy, Dollar General, Family Dollar, Rite Aid and participating 7/Eleven stores.

Credit Cards

Credit cards are widely used in the United States and the the major cards - MasterCard, Visa, American Express and Diners Club – are commonly accepted. A credit card is essential in paying for hotel accommodation or car rental. As a visitor, you may want to check about the fees levied on your card for foreign exchange transactions. While Europe and the UK have already converted to chip-and-pin credit card, the transition is still in progress in the United States. Efforts are being made to make the credit cards of most US stores compliant with chip-and-pin technology. You may find that many stores still employ the older protocols at point-of-sales. Be sure to inform your

NIAGARA FALLS TRAVEL GUIDE

bank or credit card vendor of your travel plans before leaving home.

Tourist Tax

In the United States, tourist tax varies from city to city, and can be charged not only on accommodation, but also restaurant bills, car rental and other services that cater mainly to tourists. In 22 states, some form of state wide tax is charged for accommodation and 38 states levy a tax on car rental. The city that levies the highest tax bill is Chicago. Apart from a flat fee of $2.75, you can expect to be charged 16 percent per day on hotel accommodation as well as nearly 25% for car rentals. New York charges an 18 percent hotel tax, as does Nashville, while Kansas City, Houston and Indianapolis levy around 17 percent per day hotel tax. Expect to pay 16.5 percent tax per day on your hotel bill in Cleveland and 15.6 percent per day in Seattle, with a 2 percent hike, if staying in the Seattle Tourism Improvement Area. Las Vegas charges 12 percent hotel tax. In Los Angeles, you will be charged a whopping 14 percent on your hotel room, but in Burbank, California, the rate is only 2 percent. Dallas, Texas only charges 2 percent on hotels with more than a hundred rooms. In Portland a city tax of 6 percent is added to a county tax of 5.5 percent. Do inquire about the

NIAGARA FALLS TRAVEL GUIDE

hotel tax rate in the city where you intend to stay, when booking your accommodation.

🌐 Sales Tax

In the United States, the sales tax rate is set at state level, but in most states local counties can set an additional surtax. In some states, groceries and/or prescription drugs will be exempt from tax or charged at a lower rate. There are only five states that charge no state sales tax at all. They are Oregon, Delaware, New Hampshire, Alaska and Montana. Alaska allows a local tax rate not exceeding 7 percent and in Montana, local authorities are enabled to set a surtax rate, should they wish to do so. The state sales tax is generally set at between 4 percent (Alabama, Georgia, Louisiana, and Wyoming) and 7 percent (Indiana, Mississippi, New Jersey, Tennessee, Rhode Island) although there are exceptions outside that spectrum with Colorado at 2.8 percent and California at 7.5 percent. The local surcharge can be anything from 4.7 percent (Hawaii) to around 11 percent (Oklahoma and Louisiana). Can you claim back tax on your US purchases as a tourist? In the United States, sales tax is added retro-actively upon payment, which means that it will not be included in the marked price of the goods you buy. Because it is set at state, rather than federal level, it is usually

NIAGARA FALLS TRAVEL GUIDE

not refundable.

Two states do offer sales tax refunds to tourists. In Texas you will be able to get tax back from over 6000 participating stores if the tax amount came to more than $12 and the goods were purchased within 30 days of your departure. To qualify, you need to submit the original sales receipts, your passport, flight or transport information and visa details. Refunds are made in cash, cheque or via PayPal. Louisiana was the first state to introduce tax refunds for tourists. To qualify there, you must submit all sales receipts, together with your passport and flight ticket at a Refund Center outlet.

Tipping

Tipping is very common in the United States. In sit-down restaurants, a tip of between 10 and 15 percent of the bill is customary. At many restaurants, the salaries of waiting staff will be well below minimum wage levels. With large groups of diners, the restaurant may charge a mandatory gratuity, which is automatically included in the bill. At the trendiest New York restaurants, a tip of 25 percent may be expected. While you can add a credit card tip, the best way to ensure the gratuity reaches your server is to tip separately in cash. Although tipping is less of an obligation at takeaway restaurants, such as McDonalds,

NIAGARA FALLS TRAVEL GUIDE

you can leave your change, or otherwise $1, if there is a tip jar on the counter. In the case of pizza delivery, a minimum of $3 is recommended and more is obviously appreciated. Although a delivery charge is often levied, this money usually goes to the pizzeria, rather than the driver. Tip a taxi driver 10 percent of the total fare. At your hotel, tip the porter between $1 and $2 per bag. Tip between 10 and 20 percent at hair salons, spas, beauty salons and barber shops. Tip tour guides between 10 and 20 percent for a short excursion. For a day trip, tip both the guide and the driver $5 to $10 per person, if a gratuity is not included in the cost of the tour. Tip the drivers of charter or sightseeing buses around $1 per person.

Connectivity

Mobile Phones

There are four major service providers for wireless connection in the United States. They are Verizon Wireless, T-Mobile US, AT&T Mobility and Sprint. Not all are compatible with European standards. While most countries in Europe, Asia, the Middle East and East Africa uses the GSM mobile network, only two US service providers, T-Mobile and AT&T Mobility aligns with this. Also bear in mind that GSM carriers in the United States operate using the 850 MHz/1900 MHz frequency

NIAGARA FALLS TRAVEL GUIDE

bands, whereas the UK, all of Europe, Asia, Australia and Africa use 900/1800MHz. You should check with your phone's tech specifications to find out whether it supports these standards. The other services, Verizon Wireless and Sprint use the CDMA network standard and, while Verizon's LTE frequencies are somewhat compatible with those of T-Mobile and AT&T, Sprint uses a different bandwidth for its LTE coverage.

To use your own phone, you can purchase a T-Mobile 3-in-1 starter kit for $20. If your device is unlocked, GMS-capable and supports either Band II (1900 MHz) or Band IV (1700/2100 MHz), you will be able to access the T-Mobile network. You can also purchase an AT&T sim card through the Go Phone Pay-as-you-go plan for as little as $0.99. Refill cards are available from $25 and are valid for 90 days. If you want to widen your network options, you may want to explore the market for a throwaway or disposable phone. At Walmart, you can buy non-contracted phones for as little as $9.99, as well as pre-paid sim cards and data top-up packages.

Canadians travellers will find the switch to US networks technically effortless, but should watch out for roaming costs. Several American networks do offer special international rates for calls to Canada or Mexico.

NIAGARA FALLS TRAVEL GUIDE

Dialing Code

The international dialing code for the United States is +1.

Emergency Numbers

General Emergency: 911 (this number can be used free of charge from any public phone in the United States).
MasterCard: 1-800-307-7309
Visa: 1-800-847-2911

General Information

Public Holidays

1 January: New Year's Day

3rd Monday in January: Martin Luther King Day

3rd Monday in February: President's Day

Last Monday in May: Memorial Day

4 July: Independence Day

1st Monday in September: Labour Day

2nd Monday in October: Columbus Day

11 November: Veteran's Day

4th Thursday in November: Thanksgiving Day

NIAGARA FALLS TRAVEL GUIDE

4th Friday in November: Day after Thanksgiving

25 December: Christmas Day (if Christmas Day falls on a Sunday, the Monday thereafter is a public holiday.) In some states, 26 December is a public holiday as well.

There are several festivals that are not public holidays per se, but are culturally observed in the United States. They include:

14 February: Valentine's Day

17 March: St Patrick's Day

March/April (variable): Easter or Passover

Second Sunday in May: Mother's Day

3rd Sunday in June: Father's Day

31 October: Halloween

Time Zones

The United States has 6 different time zones. **Eastern Standard Time** is observed in the states of Maine, New York, New Hampshire, Delaware, Vermont, Maryland, Rhode Island, Massachusetts, Connecticut, Pennsylvania, Ohio, North Carolina, South Carolina, Georgia, Virginia, West Virginia, Michigan, most of Florida and Indiana as well as the eastern parts of Kentucky and Tennessee. Eastern Standard Time is calculated as Greenwich Meantime/Coordinated Universal Time (UTC) -5. **Central Standard Time** is observed in Iowa, Illinois, Missouri, Arkansas, Louisiana, Oklahoma, Kansas,

NIAGARA FALLS TRAVEL GUIDE

Mississippi, Alabama, near all of Texas, the western half of Kentucky, the central and western part of Tennessee, sections of the north-western and south-western part of Indiana, most of North and South Dakota, the eastern and central part of Nebraska and the north-western strip of Florida, also known as the Florida Panhandle. Central Standard Time is calculated as Greenwich Meantime/Coordinated Universal Time (UTC) -6. **Mountain Standard Time** is observed in New Mexico, Colorado, Wyoming, Montana, Utah, Arizona, the southern and central section of Idaho, the western parts of Nebraska, South Dakota and North Dakota, a portion of eastern Oregon and the counties of El Paso and Hudspeth in Texas. Mountain Standard Time is calculated as Greenwich Meantime/Coordinated Universal Time (UTC) -7. **Pacific Standard Time** is used in California, Washington, Nevada, most of Oregon and the northern part of Idaho. Pacific Standard Time is calculated as Greenwich Meantime/Coordinated Universal Time (UTC) -8. **Alaska Standard Time** is used in Alaska and this can be calculated as Greenwich Meantime/Coordinated Universal Time (UTC) -9. Because of its distant location, Hawaii is in a time zone of its own. **Hawaii Standard Time** can be calculated as Greenwich Meantime/Coordinated Universal Time (UTC) -10.

NIAGARA FALLS TRAVEL GUIDE

🌐 Daylight Savings Time

Clocks are set forward one hour at 2.00am on the second Sunday of March and set back one hour at 2.00am on the first Sunday of November for Daylight Savings Time. The states of Hawaii and Arizona do not observe Daylight Savings Time. However, the Navajo Indian Reservation, which extends across three states (Arizona, Utah and New Mexico), does observe Daylight Savings Time throughout its lands, including that portion which falls within Arizona.

🌐 School Holidays

In the United States, the academic year begins in September, usually in the week just before or after Labour Day and ends in the early or middle part of June. There is a Winter Break that includes Christmas and New Year and a Spring Break in March or April that coincides with Easter. In some states, there is also a Winter Break in February. The summer break occurs in the 10 to 11 weeks between the ending of one academic year and the commencement of the next academic year. Holidays may vary according to state and certain weather conditions such as hurricanes or snowfall may also lead to temporary school closures in affected areas.

NIAGARA FALLS TRAVEL GUIDE

Trading Hours

Trading hours in the United States vary. Large superstores like Walmart trade round the clock at many of its outlets, or else between 7am and 10pm. Kmart is often open from 8am to 10pm, 7 days a week. Target generally opens at 8am and may close at 10 or 11pm, depending on the area. Many malls will open at 10am and close at 9pm. Expect restaurants to be open from about 11am to 10pm or 11pm, although the hours of eateries that serve alcohol and bars may be restricted by local legislation. Banking hours also vary, according to branch and area. Branches of the Bank of America will generally open at 9am, and closing time can be anywhere between 4pm and 6pm. Most post office outlets are open from 9am to 5pm on weekdays.

Driving

In the United States, motorists drive on the right hand side of the road. As public transport options are not always adequate, having access to a car is virtually essential, when visiting the United States. To drive, you will need a valid driver's licence from your own country, in addition to an international driving permit. If your driver's licence does not include a photograph, you will be asked to submit your passport for identification as well.

For car rental, you will also need a credit card. Some companies do not rent out vehicles to drivers under the age of 25. Visitors with a UK license may need to obtain a check code for rental companies, should they wish to verify the details and validity of their driver's licence, via the DVLA view-your-licence service. This can also be generated online, but must be done at least 72 hours prior to renting the car. In most cases, though, the photo card type license will be enough. The largest rental companies - Alamo, Avis, Budget, Hertz, Dollar and Thrifty - are well represented in most major cities and usually have offices at international airports. Do check about the extent of cover included in your travel insurance package and credit card agreement. Some credit card companies may include Collision Damage Waiver (CDW), which will cover you against being held accountable for any damage to the rental car, but it is recommended that you also arrange for personal accident insurance, out-of-state insurance and supplementary liability insurance. You can sometimes cut costs on car rentals by reserving a car via the internet before leaving home.

The maximum speed limit in the United States varies according to state, but is usually between 100km per hour (65 m.p.h.) and 120km per hour (75 m.p.h.). For most of the Eastern states, as

NIAGARA FALLS TRAVEL GUIDE

well as California and Oregon on the west coast the maximum speed driven on interstate highways should be 110km per hour (70 m.p.h.). Urban speed legislation varies, but in business and residential areas, speeds are usually set between 32km (20 miles) and 48km (30 miles) per hour. In Colorado, nighttime speed limits apply in certain areas where migrating wildlife could be endangered and on narrow, winding mountain passes, a limit of 32km (20 miles) per hour sometimes applies. In most American states there is a ban on texting for all drivers and a ban on all cell phone use for novice drivers.

Drinking

It is illegal in all 50 states for persons under the age of 21 to purchase alcohol or to be intoxicated. In certain states, such as Texas, persons between the age of 18 and 21 may be allowed to drink beer or wine, if in the company of a parent or legal guardian. In most states, the trading hours for establishments selling alcohol is limited. There are a few exceptions to this. In Nevada, alcohol may be sold round the clock and with few restrictions other than age. In Louisiana, there are no restrictions on trading in alcohol at state level, although some counties set their own restrictions. By contrast, Arizona has some of the strictest laws in relation to alcohol sales, consumption and driving under the influence. The sale of alcohol is prohibited on Native American reservations, unless the tribal council of that reservation has passed a vote to lift restrictions.

🌐 Smoking

There is no smoking ban set at federal level in the United States. At state level, there are 40 states in total that enact some form of state wide restriction on smoking, although the exemptions of individual states may vary. In Arizona, California, Colorado, Connecticut, Delaware, Hawaii, Illinois, Iowa, Kansas, Maine, Maryland, Massachusetts, Michigan, Minnesota, Montana, Nebraska, North Dakota, New Jersey, New Mexico, New York, Ohio, Oregon, Rhode Island, South Dakota, Utah, Vermont, Washington and Wisconsin, smoking is prohibited in all public enclosed areas, including bars and restaurants. The states of Arkansas, Florida, Indiana, Louisiana, Pennsylvania and Tennessee do have a general state wide restriction on smoking in public places, but exempt adult venues where under 21s are not allowed. This includes bars, restaurants, betting shops and gaming parlours (Indiana) and casinos (Louisiana and Pennsylvania). Nevada also has a state wide ban on smoking that exempts casinos, bars, strip clubs and brothels. In Georgia, state wide smoking legislation exempts bars and restaurants that only serve patrons over the age of 18. Idaho has a state wide ban that includes restaurants, but exempts bars serving only alcohol. New Hampshire, North Carolina and Virginia have also introduced some form of state wide smoking restriction. While the states of Alabama, Alaska, Kentucky, Mississippi, Missouri, Oklahoma, South Carolina, Texas, West Virginia and Wyoming have no state legislation, there are more specific restrictions at city and county level. In Arizona, there is an exemption for businesses located on Native American reservation and, in particular, for Native American religious ceremonies that may include smoking rituals. In California, the first state to implement anti-smoking legislation, smoking is also prohibited in parks and on sidewalks.

Electricity

Electricity: 110 volts

Frequency: 60 Hz

Electricity sockets are compatible with American Type A and Type B plugs. The Type A plug features two flat prongs or blades, while the Type B plug has the same plus an additional 'earth' prong. Most newer models of camcorders and cameras are dual voltage, which means that you should be able to charge them without an adapter in the United States, as they have a built in converter for voltage. You may find that appliances from the UK or Europe which were designed to accommodate a higher voltage will not function as effectively in the United

States. While a current converter or transformer will be able to adjust the voltage, you may still experience some difficulty with the type of devices that are sensitive to variations in frequency as the United States uses 60 Hz, instead of the 50 Hz which is common in Europe and the UK. Appliances like hairdryers will usually be available in hotels and since electronic goods are fairly cheap in the United States, the easiest strategy may be to simply purchase a replacement. Bear in mind, that you may need an adaptor or transformer to operate it once you return home.

Food & Drink

Hamburgers, hot dogs and apple pie may be food items that come to mind when considering US culinary stereotypes, but Americans eat a wide variety of foods. They love steaks and ribs when dining out and pancakes or waffles for breakfast. As a society which embraces various immigrant communities, America excels at adopting and adapting traditional staples and adding its own touch to them. Several "Asian" favorites really originated in the United States. These include the California roll (offered in sushi restaurants) and the fortune cookie (chinese). Popular Hispanic imports include tacos, enchiladas and burritos. Another stereotype of American cuisine is large portion sizes. Hence the existence of American inventions such as the footlong sub, the footlong chilli cheese hot dog and the Krispy Creme burger, which combines a regular hamburger with a donut. Corn dogs are fairground favorites. Most menus are more balanced however. It is common to ask for a doggy bag (to take away remaining food) in a restaurant.

When in the South, enjoy corn bread, grits and southern fried chicken. Try spicy buffalo wings in New York, traditionally prepared baked beans in Boston and deep dish pizza in Chicago. French fries are favorites with kids of all ages, but Americans also love their potatoes as hash browns or the bite sized tater tots. Indulge your sweet tooth with Twinkies, pop tarts, cup cakes and banana splits. Popular sandwiches include the BLT (bacon, lettuce, tomato, the Reuben sandwich, the sloppy joe and the peanut butter and jelly.

Sodas (fizzy drinks) and bottled waters are the top beverages in the United States. The top selling soft drinks are Coca Cola, followed by Pepsi Cola, Diet Coke, Mountain Dew and Dr Pepper. In America's colonial past, tea was initially the hot beverage of choice and it was tea politics that kicked off the American Revolution, but gradually tea has been replaced by coffee in popularity. From the 1970s, Starbucks popularized coffee culture in the United States. Americans still drink gallons of tea and they are particularly fond of a refreshing glass of iced tea. Generally, Americans drink more beer than wine and favorite brands include Bud Light, followed by Coors Light, Budweiser and Miller Light. Popular cocktails are the Martini, the Manhattan, the Margarita, the Bloody Mary, the Long Island Ice tea and Sex on the Beach.

American Sports

Baseball is widely regarded as the national sport of America. The sport originated in the mid 1800s and superficially shares the basic objective of cricket, which is to score runs by hitting a ball pitched by the opposing team, but in baseball, the innings ends as soon as three players have been caught out. A point is scored when a runner has passed three bases and reached the 4th or home base of the baseball diamond. After 9 innings, the team with the highest number of runs is declared the winner. The Baseball World Series is played in the fall (autumn), usually in October, and consists of best-of-seven play-off between the two top teams representing the rival affiliations of the National League and American League.

Although the origins of American football can be found in rugby, the sport is now widely differentiated from its roots and today numerous distinctions exist between the two. In American football, a game is divided into four quarters, with each team fielding 11 players, although unlimited substitution is allowed.

NIAGARA FALLS TRAVEL GUIDE

Players wear helmets and heavy padding as any player can be tackled, regardless of ball possession. An annual highlight is the Super Bowl, the championship game of the National Football League. The event is televised live to over a 100 million viewers and features a high profile halftime performance by a top music act. Super bowl Sunday traditionally takes place on the first Sunday of February.

The roots of stock car racing can be found in America's prohibition era, when bootleggers needed powerful muscle cars (often with modifications for greater speed) to transport their illicit alcohol stocks. Informal racing evolved to a lively racing scene in Daytona, Florida. An official body, NASCAR, was founded in 1948 to regulate the sport, NASCAR. Today, NASCAR racing has millions of fans. One of its most prestigious events is the Sprint Cup, a championship which comprises of 36 races and kicks off each year with the Daytona 500.

Rodeo originated from the chores and day-to-day activities of Spanish cattle farmers and later, the American ranchers who occupied the former Spanish states such as Texas, California and Arizona. The advent of fencing eliminated the need for cattle drives, but former cowboys found that their skills still offered good entertainment, providing a basis for wild west shows such as those presented by Buffalo Bill. Soon, rodeo events became the highlight of frontier towns throughout the west. During the first half of the 20th centuries, organizations formed to regulate events. Today, rodeo is considered a legitimate national sport with millions of fans. If you want to experience the thrill of this extreme sport, attend one of its top events. The Prescott Frontier Days show in Arizona is billed to be America's oldest rodeo. The Reno Rodeo in Nevada is a 10 day event that takes place in mid-June and includes the option of closer participation as a volunteer. Rodeo Houston, a large 20 day event that takes place towards the end of winter, is coupled to a livestock show. Visit the San Antonio show in Texas during February for the sheer variety of events. The National Western Rodeo in Denver Colorado is an indoor event that attracts up to half a million spectators each year. The National Finals that takes place in Las Vegas during December is the prestigious championship that marks the end of the year's rodeo calendar.

Useful Websites

https://esta.cbp.dhs.gov/esta/ -- The US Electronic System for Travel Authorization
http://www.visittheusa.com/
http://roadtripusa.com/
http://www.roadtripamerica.com/

NIAGARA FALLS TRAVEL GUIDE

http://www.road-trip-usa.info/

http://www.autotoursusa.com/

http://www.onlyinyourstate.com/

http://www.theamericanroadtripcompany.co.uk/

Made in the USA
Monee, IL
10 August 2022